SO-BZA-845

395

H 36498

How the Animals Do It

How the Animals Do It

written and illustrated by

Larry Feign

Souvenir Press

In memory of
Queequeg, Damsel, Blue, Spot, Clown
and Jimmy

Copyright © 1992 by Larry Feign

First published in the USA by
Barricade Books Inc, Fort Lee, NJ

First British edition published 1992 by
Souvenir Press Ltd., 43 Great Russell Street,
London WC1B 3PA

All Rights Reserved. No part of this publication
may be reproduced, stored in a retrieval system,
or transmitted, in any form or by any means, electronic,
mechanical, photocopying, recording or otherwise, without
the prior permission of the Copyright owner

ISBN 0 285 63111 X

Printed in Great Britain by
St Edmundsbury Press Ltd, Bury St Edmunds, Suffolk

Contents

A Brief History of Sex

Why is there sex? Besides, that is, to have something to lie about in locker rooms. The answer is: no one knows, but hey, who's complaining? After all, what would this world be like without sex? We'd have nothing to daydream about at school or in the office. Hollywood would have to rely exclusively on violence. The entire country of France would be superfluous.

In the scale of things, sex is a relatively recent invention. The world got along without it just fine, thank you, for thousands of millions of years.

The first single-celled animals reproduced by cloning: that is, splitting in half. Mother and daughter (or father and son) were also identical twins. But after two billion years of cloning, apparently everyone was getting rather bored. So, a few hundred million years ago, a new craze hit the oceans: genetic swapping. Some single-celled organisms—probably teenaged ones—discovered that it was more fun to inject their chromosomes into one another before splitting.

Eventually a few got hooked, and couldn't reproduce without genetic interaction. Like true addicts, they developed a craving for it, which has been passed down through trillions of generations to you and me. All creatures great and small are now born with the overpowering drive to reproduce.

Just why sex evolved is still a mystery. A leading theory explains that gene-swapping was faster than waiting around to mutate. Though after two billion years of surviving just fine with a new mutation every few centuries, one wonders where the sudden hurry came from.

The reasons against sex ever gaining popularity are formidable. For one thing, if the goal is to produce heirs, then sexual reproduction is probably the least efficient way to go about it. The original method—cloning—works so well that a single microscopic bacterium could theoretically be responsible for enough offspring to create a mass greater than the planet Jupiter in

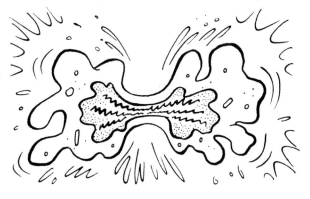

about four days, something not even the Osmond Family could hope to match.

Secondly, it's a burden on everybody. A clone can go off and pursue its own career the instant it's born. But babies produced by sexual means are tiny and vulnerable, and make attractive snacks for hungry neighbours. They need either to be reared and defended by their parents, or produced in such prodigious numbers that at least a few will remain after most of their siblings have been consumed like so many pretzel sticks.

What's more, sex is an enormous waste of time, energy and natural resources. The manufacture of millions of fresh sperm every day, or incubating a foetus for weeks or months, are an extravagant waste compared to the old system of cloning and having the rest of the day off.

Consider how many raw materials are invested in the construction and maintenance of bodily accessories solely devoted to mating. A deer's antlers, a peacock's tail feathers, a woman's stiletto heels, are enormous burdens which slow down their owners and make them vulnerable to predators, such as wolves, warthogs and construction workers.

Mating competitions among suitors, courtship rituals, and the need to copulate again and again to ensure that an egg is fertilised, all take up a lot of time and energy. Not to mention all the money that's wasted on dinner dates, satin sheets, edible panties, and other necessities of the breeding process.

With so much going against it, it's a wonder that sex evolved at all.

Our early sea-dwelling forebears had it easy: male and female simply spewed their eggs and sperm into the water, and as long as they drifted reasonably close to one another, fertilisation occurred.

But once animals started moving onto dry land, they encountered a number of tricky problems. They could no longer reproduce by ejaculating or ovulating anywhere they pleased. Even if they aimed straight at each other—besides being messy and somewhat rude—the embryos quickly dried up in the sun.

Eggs were the answer. A secure package inside which an embryo could remain wet and

grow. They also made perfect breakfast fare. So they had to be protected, as well as kept warm.

Thus, with sex came sexism. Females assumed responsibility for incubating and protecting the eggs, plus defending and training the new babies. Meanwhile, male consciousness never developed beyond spewing their semen and then splitting the scene, behaviour that can still be found today in summer beach romances and sailors on leave.

Eventually, a few mother reptiles started keeping their eggs inside until after fertilisation. But this meant the sperm had to get in somehow. Luckily, males had the foresight to have developed penises a few million years before. Finally they got to learn how much fun it was to use them.

Sexual intercourse was later refined to a high art by mammals, but the basic principle remains the same. For millions of years there have been no new major developments in sex; that is, until the advent of '0898' numbers.

Today, the lives of all living creatures revolve around breeding. A bizarre variety of courtship and mating behaviours has evolved, each for specific reasons of survival and convenience.

Many of the animals we all know and love do the weirdest things. Your parents probably never realised this when they nervously mumbled about 'the birds and the bees'. If only they knew the real story!

That's what this book is about. Everything you are about to read is true. Yes, our winged, furry, gilled, scaled, slimy and creepy cousins actually do these things!

One final note of warning: DO NOT TRY THESE ACTIONS AT HOME.

Remember, the animals performing them are professionals.

How Fifty Animals
DO IT

Alligators
The original Deep Throat

Alligators don't get by on good looks alone. Every male has to be a song-and-dance man too.

Males engage in loud bellowing mating duels, in which the guy with the deepest, most thunderous roar wins. The successful crooner then performs a 'water dance'. Guttural low-frequency humming deep in his abdomen makes the water around him rise in a fine mist of tiny dancing droplets.

Not just the swamp is set aquiver. A female staked out nearby is attracted by the vibrations in the water, and approaches her reptilian Romeo.

The courting pair climbs ashore and starts wrestling, forcing each others' heads under water. At last, the male wraps himself around his beloved for thirty seconds of conjugal bliss.

Then, of course, it's 'See you later, alligator.'

Anglerfish
Till death do us part

Males of this deep sea species are thousands of times smaller than the females. A young male in heat, or perhaps several, will bite a female with fanglike teeth near her genital orifice ... and then never leave!

Having bitten on, his lips and tongue fuse with her flesh. Gradually, his circulation and bodily systems merge with hers, and his own organs—including heart, stomach and brain—degenerate. All except the gonads, that is! Eventually he dissolves into nothing more than an attached male sex organ.

Rather like some of the guys my sister used to date.

Bacteria
Microorganism microorgasm

Even microbes need a little action now and then.

All a single-celled bacterium has to do to reproduce is split into two. But this can get awfully lonely sometimes.

Often two microbes will nudge up to each other and one will send a small protrusion penetrating into the other. Through this 'tube' connecting their bodies, each donates chromosomes to the other, after which they separate.

When each partner later divides into two, the offspring carry the new chromosome mixture.

Then all the relatives come over and argue about whether it's got her nucleus and his ectoplasm, or his flagella and her double helix.

Barnacles
Going to great lengths

Barnacles are the most well-endowed of all creatures: their penises are *forty* times as long as their bodies.

What's more, they all have one. Barnacles are hermaphroditic, having both female and male sex organs. They can fertilise themselves if necessary, but prefer not to.

Since barnacles are stationary, they let their penises do the walking. The organ emerges from the shell and gropes around the surrounding rocks until it contacts a potential partner. If no resistance is met, in it goes. The partner may then reciprocate.

It must feel awfully good, considering the ejaculation needed to shoot sperm all that length!

Bats
Fly-by-night affairs

Bats do it in the air. At least they try to.

In-flight copulation is a clumsy affair, and some couples end up tumbling to the ground during the attempt. However, it's made easier by the fact that the male has a very long penis. Kind of like jets refuelling in-flight.

Mating takes place in late autumn, just before the colony goes into hibernation. After mating, the sperm remain dormant inside the female until spring, when she finally ovulates. To make sure enough sperm survive the winter, she needs a large supply. Therefore, a female always takes more than one willing bat-man into her belfry.

Bears
Do it in the woods

Bears are antisocial, except when it comes to mating. Both sexes are highly promiscuous lovers.

A chance encounter in the woods, perhaps a shared stolen picnic basket in the moonlight ... and one thing leads to another. A couple will remain together for several days of intense sexual activity, then go their separate ways again. Rather like a Hollywood marriage. Each may have several such affairs over the course of the spring.

Bears start becoming sexually active at four years of age. Which could explain what Goldilocks was doing in Baby Bear's bed!

Bees
All the Queen's men

Of the 50,000 residents in a typical honeybee colony, just two get all the fun.

The queen rules over tens of thousands of female workers, who are sterile, and a private harem of a few drone males, who do nothing but sit around waiting to make whoopee with Her Majesty.

One spring day, the queen leads her male consorts out of the hive. After finding a suitable mating spot, she selects one drone, who impregnates her while the others watch.

Once her thousands of eggs are laid, the males are no longer needed. At the end of the summer, all are ejected from the hive and die!

What a way to buzz off.

Cats
The original sex kittens

When cats are in heat, the whole world knows.

The neighbourhood tomcats gather round to serenade their feline *femmes* with whiny rasping

choruses. The toms scratch and fight and spray anything—and anyone—nearby to mark individual territory. Then the females pick and choose.

During sex, too, everyone yowls a lot. At first it may be out of pleasure, but then . . .

A tomcat's penis is covered with tiny hooks, angled not to hurt the female on the way in. But as he ejaculates and withdraws, the hooks scrape at her insides, triggering ovulation. They also trigger a blood-curdling, bone-tingling scream. As well as a nasty swipe of female claws across male face and yet another screech.

See what fun your kitty's missing when you get him or her fixed?

Chimpanzees
Real swingers

Chimpanzees don't fool around when it comes to fooling around!

Both sexes are highly promiscuous. Males have enormous testicles to produce the voluminous quantities of sperm expended in their daily frolics.

But when they're not busy fornicating, the sexes remain apart. Adult females gather in groups. Feminine bonding consists of playing with each other and rubbing their genitals together. Mothers even do this with their own daughters!

The adult males, meanwhile, stay at home with the children. What nice guys, you think . . . until you find out that Dad's babysitting activities include fondling the sex organs of both his daughters and his sons.

I've heard of going ape over your own children, but this goes too far.

Cockroaches
Sex among the silverware

Judging by their numbers in some restaurant kitchens, cockroaches do it quite often and with gusto.

They like to do it in the dark—behind the refrigerator, in your garbage can, or on top of your dishes in the cupboard. A male climbs on top of a female from behind, inserts his little roach-penis, and is finished in a few seconds.

Soon afterwards, the female lays hundreds of fertilised eggs, encased *en masse* in a hard brown sack. She carries the sack around like a purse for several days, eventually depositing it in a safe place, where the babies finally hatch.

But do Beverly Hills roaches carry *designer* purses?

Cuckoos
Who's been sleeping in <u>my</u> clock?

American cuckoo birds, like a lot of Americans, could use marriage counsellors.

They pair up as monogamous couples for the

breeding season, but the honeymoon doesn't last long. While the husband is out gathering materials for the nest, another male will commonly come along and mate with the lonely wife, then dash off before the man of the house returns. Whence the term *cuckold*.

This rarely leads to divorce, however. They may be cuckoo, but they're not bird-brained enough to have invented lawyers!

Deer
Horny . . . or is it <u>antlery</u>?

A stag uses his antlers not only for defence, but also for debauchery.

Come August, the males of the herd begin their annual jousting for feminine attention. The

fights can be ferocious. The winning stag dominates a harem for a few weeks, mating with each female several times before wandering off for new adventures.

And what of the losers? They too get their pleasure. Many stags are able to masturbate with their antlers! As he strokes the sensitive tips on a nearby bush, his penis becomes erect and ejaculates, all within five seconds. A particularly virile stag may masturbate several times a day, even after mating.

It's no wonder that in Asia, deer antlers are considered an aphrodisiac (though deer testicles are cheaper, since they're under a buck!).

Dogs
Screwed in tight

When dogs do it, nothing can tear them apart.

Once a male goes in, he can't pull out. A dog's penis has special folds on it. When it becomes erect, the folds fan out, like the threads on a screw, holding him firmly in place in the female's vagina until the act is finished.

Premature retraction can cause severe pain and lesions, or may even fracture the penis. Not to mention what it would do to *her* insides.

Clearly, the Early Withdrawal Method is not an option for Fido and FiFi.

Dragonflies
I dig you, baby

Dragonflies use hardware as sex aids.

They also mate while in flight. The male flies ahead of the female, grasping her head between his hind legs, while she curls her abdomen forward to receive him.

His penis is shaped like a miniature shovel. He uses it first to scoop out her genital orifice, to

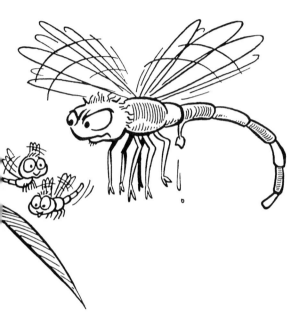

remove any rival's semen that may be there. Then he squirts his own sperm onto the end of the shovel and packs it into her.

Another male may come right along and repeat the same. The more sex partners a female has, the longer she postpones pregnancy. Promiscuity clearly has its own rewards.

Ducks
Bad birds

Ducks are the only animal species, besides humans, which practices rape.

Actually, ducks are monogamous. They choose their mates in late autumn and remain together throughout the year.

Mating takes place out on the pond. Floating together, the male mounts the female from behind. When they're finished, they climb ashore to build a nest.

Meanwhile, a number of unmated males lurk about on shore looking for a piece of action. The act of rape is violent and humiliating. The female victim is pursued by a gang of rogue males, who chase and peck at her until she is exhausted. One attacker then grabs her neck between his jaws, wrenching her head back while he violates her. Then another assailant takes over. She can be severely wounded by the time her ordeal is through.

Isn't it about time someone *quacked* down on such behaviour?

Earthworms
Love thy neighbour

Worms have it both ways. They're hermaph-roditic: both female *and* male. So, it doesn't

matter whom they mate with—it's always a perfect match! A worm cannot fertilise itself, though.

Earthworms like to do it with the boy—or is it girl?—next door. On a mild, damp night, a couple of neighbours come part-way out of their lairs and lie head-to-toe on the moist ground. They stay connected for three to four hours, squirting sticky semen over each other from grooves in their sides. Later, when they're alone, each secretes eggs, which are fertilised in the sticky sperm mass on their flanks.

Don't you wish your neighbours were that friendly?

Elephants
Tickle my ivories

Elephants may be big and tough, but they have a nose for nookie.

In the still of the evening, love blossoms. Males and females seek each other out among the trees and bushes. A he and she-elephant who have caught each other's eyes signal mutual interest by trumpeting a brief, special note back and forth.

If they like what they hear, they move on to foreplay. Snuggling up side-by-side, the courting pair caresses one another with their trunks. Gradually, trunks intertwine and they place them in each other's mouths and gently lick the sensitive tips. After a few such passes, the male moves behind his partner and mounts her.

Now *that's* heavy petting!

Fireflies
Light my fire

That's more than just a light show in the mid-summer fields and tall grasses—it's an insect singles bar gone wild!

Fireflies are males with fires in their bellies. When they're in a courting mood, a chemical in the abdomen makes them emit a greenish light. This draws the attention of glow-worms, their flightless female counterparts. The latter live in

the grass, but they too put on a glow when aroused.

Thousands of males at a time hover around, flashing mating signals. When a female sees a light pattern she likes, she climbs up onto a leaf and blinks her own signal in response. The nearest male is then on her in a flash. In fact, males are so quick to respond to a flashing signal, they've even been known to mate with a blinking penlight!

Frogs
Horny toads

Some frogs will do it with *anything!*

When he's in the mood, a male clasps any object he comes into contact with. If he grabs another male, the victim chirps to tell Romeo to let go. But breeding females remain quiet. Therefore, anything he latches onto that stays silent is perceived as female, and receives the benefit of his hormones. This can include other frog species, fish, plants, rubbish ... even an extended human finger (try it some time)!

Normally, though, he just sits in his corner of the pond with his buddies, chirping deep mating calls. The local females come along to check out the guys, and each selects her partner.

She taps him to signal interest and he grabs on. No penetration is involved; as she releases her eggs, he simultaneously deposits sperm on top.

That is, if he isn't already previously engaged with a discarded beer bottle.

Fruitflies
Apples and oranges . . . and other forbidden fruits

A male fruitfly hums when he's in heat ... but not with his mouth; that organ he saves for other activities.

When he spots an attractive female, he woos her by vibrating his wings to a low-pitched hum, inaudible to human hearing, but which she picks up through her antennae.

If she is suitably impressed (assuming she enjoys his taste in music), she adopts a passive posture and invites him to lick her genitals. Which he does with relish, before finally mounting her.

Now you know where all that giggling behind the fruit basket comes from!

Giraffes
It's not the measure, it's the motion

A giraffe's neck isn't the only thing that's extra-long!

A male giraffe's penis when aroused hangs down below his knees: from four to five feet in length. That may look good to the girls, but for the poor guy, some minor acrobatics are necessary in the act of love-making.

Like other hoofed animals, they do it standing up. The male mounts his beloved from behind, but his lengthy appendage can't rise to the required angle on its own. Thus, with a few deft flips of the hips, he sends it swinging like a pendulum. As it finally reaches the desired height, with precision timing he thrusts his pelvis forward.

The female's moan of delight can be heard halfway across the savannah.

Horses
No horsing around

A horse's sex life is nothing to bet on.

In the natural scheme of things, horses mate in harems. During the breeding season, the stallions in a herd fight each other over a bevy of mares. The herd then splits into several harems, and the lucky males and most of the females have a good time for a week or two.

Poor domesticated horses, though! The best breeding studs are stabled alone, forbidden conjugal visits because of their hot tempers. And no wonder they're mad: breeding is arranged by the owner, who shoves an enormous syringe up the stud's penis to relieve him of his sperm, which is then likewise squirted into a selected mare.

It's a system most horses would prefer to buck.

Kangaroos
Lie me kangaroo down, sport

Contrary to the obvious pun potential, kangaroos do not 'hop' on each other for sex. Actually, she crouches on all fours and he does it 'in the outback'.

Males box one another during mating contests. Winners get to mate with several females in the group. But losers needn't worry: they'll get another chance quicker than they can say 'didgeridoo.'

Kangaroo foetuses don't remain inside for long. After only a few weeks in the womb, the immature joey crawls out of the vagina and up into mother's pouch, where it continues its gestation. Several days later, mother is all ready to mate again.

And the guys? They—what else?—jump for joy!

Lions
Of royal breeding

Like proper royalty, the king and queen of beasts link families rather than individuals.

Within a pride of lions, each generation of

females consists of sisters and cousins. When their male relations—also brothers and cousins—mature, they are ejected from the group. They roam around as a pack, seeking to join another pride whose young males have also recently taken leave.

When these hot-headed cats move in with a group of lonely sisters, first they drive out the girls' adolescent brothers, then they kill all the young cubs. Rather than fighting to protect their babies, the slaughter sets the lionesses' hormones alight, and carnage quickly turns into carnality.

It gives new meaning to the term *bloodlust*.

Mice and Rats
A whole lotta shakin' going on

Mice and rats love to do it. Under ideal conditions, a single couple could have *twenty million* descendants after only three years!

A female mouse gets to enjoy herself more than most animals. She is by no means monogamous. In fact, a pregnant female who finds herself in close quarters with an unfamiliar male will have a spontaneous abortion, then go right into heat again!

Their cousins the rats, on the other hand, aren't so easy-going. After copulation, a substance in the semen coagulates in the female's vagina, forming a hard chastity plug.

It would appear that rats and mice are as divided as the US Supreme Court on the issue of women's reproductive rights.

Minks
Once is enough

Minks do it full-length.

These furry weasel-like animals breed only once a year, but they make it last. The male mink latches his jaws onto the female's neck and locks his four legs around her body. They make plenty of noise while copulating, which keeps the neighbours up all night. One act of coitus can last for as long as eight hours!

They probably spend the rest of the year catching their breath.

Mosquitoes
Stay away from my gal, sucker

Mosquitoes are the jealous type.

The male mounts the female from behind. To ensure that his mate remains faithful, his semen contains an anti-aphrodisiac: a substance which reduces her receptivity to other males, as well as other males' attraction to her.

After sex, a female's thoughts turn to food. She needs a meal of fresh blood in order to ripen her eggs before she lays them in the nearest stagnant pool.

So, next time you get poked, have sympathy, remember, she probably just got poked herself.

Mules
Sigh...

Mules don't do it.

Octopus
At arm's length

Octopi pay an arm and a leg for sex.

When he's ready to mate, a male octopus releases a tubular leatherlike sac filled with sperm. He grabs hold of it with one of his arms and shoves it into the genital orifice of his female partner.

Then his arm falls off.

It detaches from his body and serves as a plug to hold the sperm sac in place. Don't worry, he grows back a new arm later.

As any cephalopod will tell you: better a broken limb than a broken heart.

Penguins
Cool about sex

In the Antarctic, things don't really get hot until it's down to 70 degrees (Fahrenheit) below zero.

During the long winter nights, penguins pair off. A male courts his sweetheart by offering gifts: a shiny stone, or (if he's cheap) a piece of snow. If she accepts, the couple remain together for the rest of the breeding season.

She lays a single egg. He fertilises it, then tucks it between the top of his foot and the fat of his overhanging belly to keep it warm. He stands still in one spot, neither moving nor eating, for six weeks at a stretch, while his mate is free to do as she pleases.

Talk about a sensitive new age type of guy!

Pigs
By the hairs of their chinny-chin-chins

For pigs, the fun is all in the foreplay.

A male charms his mate by foaming at the mouth and grinding his teeth while poking his snout up between her hind legs. An especially amorous boar will even lift his sow's hindquarters off the ground. All the while he hums a mating song of rhythmic, low-pitched grunts.

The sow returns his affection by nuzzling her he-hog's scrotum and genitals. She may even try to mount him.

Finally, she gets into mating posture, standing totally rigid while the male climbs on and copulates.

Next time you eat pork rinds, remember: someone else has recently been nibbling there.

Pigeons
Cooing wooing

Pigeons are the old-fashioned types.

A gentleman introduces himself to an attractive ladybird by bowing grandly and cooing in his deepest voice. If she's suitably charmed, she returns the gesture with a dainty bow, while coyly lowering her beak.

Their caressing, too, is genteel. He nuzzles her. She runs her beak through his feathers. He strokes her in return. At last they kiss: beaks together, they sip a sweet mead produced in each other's throats.

After minutes or even hours of heavy petting, they are whipped up to a soaring passion. She crouches, he mounts her from behind, and they consummate the relationship.

That is, if the parkbench they're under isn't already occupied by humans doing the same.

Porcupines
You give me pins and needles

Porcupines get straight to the point.

A male in heat chases females after dark. When he's found one he likes (most likely the sharpest dresser), he gets in front of her and flirts by flicking the quills on his back up and down.

If she doesn't run away, he lifts his tail and douses her with a squirt of urine to mark her as his.

Then he mounts her. How he does so without injury is still a mystery to science.

Praying Mantises
I lost my head over you

Female praying mantises do more than just turn men's heads—they *eat* them.

When he spots an available female, a male freezes, sometimes for hours, then slowly and cautiously approaches. At last, he grabs her from behind and beats her head with his antennae while he humps up and down. Copulation can last thirty minutes.

While he's thus engaged, she reaches round and eats his head! But, undiscouraged, the now headless mantis loses all inhibition and mates with abandon, thrusting with extra fervour. In fact, some species are unable to release their sperm until the head is devoured!

Occasionally, if a female spots a male first, she may ambush him and eat his head before he's even mounted her. Nevertheless, he will still instinctively move round, mount and copulate.

Perhaps he should have taken her out to dinner first.

Rabbits
Do the bunny hop

Rabbits breed like . . . well, rabbits.

It's not that they have libidos as big as their ears. It's that they get off to an early start. A

rabbit or hare reaches sexual maturity at around four months of age.

Like porcupines, a male rabbit marks the bunny of his choice by dashing in front of her, lifting his tail and squirting a shot of urine at her.

Then of course he hops on top of her.

Salamanders
Philander salamander

Never date a salamander. You never know who you may end up with.

Salamanders don't have intercourse. A male courts a female by walking directly ahead of her and wagging his tail in her face. If she's interested, she nudges her head against his rear end. That's his signal to release a sac of sperm from his genital opening onto the ground. As they continue walking, the female passes over the sperm sac. When it contacts her genitals it sticks on and does its job.

Some salamanders cheat. A second male may come along and butt in between a courting couple. The intruder tricks the original male by mimicking female behaviour: he nudges the first male's behind, making the first male release his sperm. Then the interloper releases his own sperm right on top. When the female passes over, she gets only the top sperm sac. The first guy never even knew what happened!

Now you know where soap operas steal their plot ideas.

Sea Slugs
Single file sex

Sea slugs literally line up for sex.

Like their land-based cousins, sea slugs are hermaphroditic: everyone has both male and female genitalia. But they are certainly not monogamous. They begin with one acting the male and mounting his partner from behind. Then a third participant slides up at the rear and joins in the fun. A fourth meanwhile mounts the third-in-line, and so on.

Lines of five or six are common, and copulation chains of *twenty* or more have been known.

It makes for some interesting party games!

Seahorses
Subaquatic role reversal

A female seahorse sticks it to the male, and *he* gets pregnant!

An ovulating sea-mare wastes no time. She grabs a nearby stallion with her tail and leads him in a swaying courtship dance up to the water's surface.

Once there, she extends a special appendage, through which she discharges her eggs into a pouch on the male's belly. He releases sperm within his pouch. And there inside Daddy the eggs incubate until hundreds of little sea-foals come galloping out.

But which does he apply for: maternity or paternity leave?

Seals
Seal without a kiss

Each spring, seals gather on the beach for the biggest bash of the year. And we do mean <u>bash</u>.

Males engage in fierce mating battles. They rush headlong at each other, tearing at their rivals with their teeth, covering one another with bloody scars.

For the winners, though, the rewards are unparalleled. A victorious male gains exclusive rights to mate with the entire bevy of females who gather on his corner of the beach.

One at a time, the bull seal embraces a partner from behind and nibbles her neck as he makes love to her. Coitus lasts around fifteen minutes and may be repeated several times with each of his several partners.

It's an exhausting job, but *someone* has to do it!

Sheep
So <u>that's</u> what they mean by horny

The sheep mating season is a real bang. Late in the year, rams engage in head-butting contests to win dominance over the females in the flock.

The most spectacular mating duels occur among Bighorn Sheep. Bighorn rams live in separate flocks from the ewes. Their duels are so furious that the clashing of their enormous horns echoes throughout the high mountains. The champion cranium-crasher gets to join the female flock and ram it in as many ewes as he pleases.

That is, if a shepherd hasn't got to them first.

Sloths
Too laid back to get laid

Three-toed sloths do it, well . . . *slothfully*.

The closest these sleepy (average 19 hours a day) tree-hangers come to carnality is when, about once a year, a female wakes up with a mild itch to scratch and cries out: 'Aieee!' A nearby male is aroused—if that's the word for it—from

his slumber and slowly, silently descends from his branch to meet his equally sluggish partner in the tall grass below.

Courtship is brief, unemotional and apathetic. The couple basically lie together in a belly-to-belly embrace for half an hour or so. What passes for climax is a few brief muscle spasms. Then they drift apart and back to sleep.

If this sounds like your marriage, then maybe you need to consult a zoologist!

Slugs
A sticky affair

Slugs are the only species for whom being a slimeball is a social advantage.

Slugs are hermaphroditic: each has a retracted penis near the front of the body and a vagina in the middle. To get pregnant, though, one needs a partner.

Foreplay takes place high up on a leaf or branch. The courting couple does a circle dance, oozing slimy mucus all over each other. Encased in this gelatinous mass, they drop into space, suspended from the branch by a sticky thread of slime.

Dangling in the air, they twist round and eat the mucus off one another's bodies. Finally, they coil together and spew gooey globs of sperm over each other's vaginal openings. Then they climb back up the slime rope and go their separate ways.

I wonder what they do when they want to get *kinky?*

Snails
Keep your feelers to yourself, you slime

Snails' penises come out of the sides of their heads. Not only that ... everyone has one. Snails, like slugs, are hermaphroditic, with both female and male sexual organs.

A snail can't impregnate itself, though. But any two snails of the same species can mate with each other, which sure makes dating simpler.

When mating a couple latch together by stabbing built-in hooks into one another. Then they extend their long, snake-like penises out of their temples and into each others' vaginas.

Is it any wonder French people eat these creatures?

Snakes
Double your pleasure...

A male snake has a double penis. Lucky guy. Unfortunately, he can use only one at a time.

A snake boy and girl court one another by rearing up face-to-face, then dancing and swaying for several minutes or even several hours. If each is sufficiently charmed by the other, they intertwine, the male coiling himself around his partner. Depending upon which side of him her vagina faces, either the left or right spur of his penis emerges and copulation takes place.

And you thought snakes only had forked *tongues!*

Spiders
Your web or mine?

Spiders do it manually.

Producing heirs to the web is a complex task. First the male spins a special web onto which he deposits a droplet of semen from his genital opening. He then draws the sperm into a syringe-like device on one of his legs, and creeps off in search of a mate.

He approaches his potential partner with extreme caution. Most female spiders are many times larger than males and often mistake the latter for prey, even while mating. To avoid becoming a post-coital snack, some males first bind the female in silken threads. Tarantula males use special hooks to clamp their tarantulette's mouth

open. And you can guess where the Black Widow gets her name.

Once in position, the male inserts his sperm-syringe into the partner and squirts. Then he runs like hell!

Starfish
The Milky Way

Starfish are into group sex.

A female sheds her eggs into the surrounding water, and in doing so, triggers a mating frenzy. When one female starts spewing eggs, other females in the area are stimulated to do the same, while the local males release clouds of semen.

In the resulting carnal soup, eggs are fertilised and larvae form. This mass orgy may even be touched off by a female being accidentally crushed or squeezed.

Starfish can also reproduce by breaking off limbs. When one of either sex loses an append-age, a new arm grows in its place. At the same time, a new starfish also grows from the severed arm. Talk about a real chip off the old block!

Swans
Dull birds

Lawyers hate swans.

These big birds are strictly monogamous and mate for life, with a divorce rate of under one per cent. They enjoy their marriages, too, normally waiting two or three years after pairing up before having children. Even 'remarried' widows or widowers wait several years after their second marriage to breed.

The day the long honeymoon is finally over, the husband gently caresses his darling's head and neck while whispering soft, sweet cries in her ear, then moves behind her and . . . well, gives her his goose.

Then along come the baby cygnets and the family lives together happily ever after. No wonder fairy tales are full of swans rather than ducks (see the entry for 'Ducks').

Tropical Fish
Boys will be girls

Tropical reef fish are the original trans-sexuals.

Many species of marine fish gather harems, over which a few males fight for dominance. The losers either leave the area, or they join the group . . . and become female! They change coloration, develop female sexual organs and produce eggs like everybody else.

Females normally lay eggs in nests in the coral, where they are later fertilised. The male may find himself having to ejaculate sperm every thirty seconds to accommodate all the females in his group.

For the harem boss, the constant effort of

fighting rivals, performing courtship displays and spawning with dozens of mates is exhausting. If he weakens or dies and no other male comes along to take his place, the largest female in the harem assumes the role: she becomes a he!

Imagine the mood swings from all those hormonal changes.

Turtles
Knock! Knock! Who's there?

Turtles and tortoises don't come out of their shells when they make love.

They mate just once a year. After a bit of male jousting for the attention of a female, a he-turtle mounts the she-turtle from behind. Shortly thereafter, she lays her eggs in the sand.

A few species go a bit farther. A female Box Turtle plays coy; the male has to knock on her shell to coax her into opening up for him.

On the other hand, male turtles of southern Europe and North Africa won't countenance such behaviour. He mounts his female in the water and wounds or even drowns her if she resists. Which goes to show that the machismo culture of those regions is not limited to one species.

Whales
Wham-bam-thank-you-ma'am

Giant blue whales (and, reportedly, other whale species) do it with a splash.

In springtime, a young leviathan's thoughts turn to love. With songs and balletic dancing and swimming movements, they charm and woo one another, sometimes turning on their sides and rubbing flippers together.

To consummate the relationship, the whale couple leap out of the water into the air, slapping

against each other. In that all-too-brief moment, copulation takes place.

It must be pretty good, though, considering they migrate thousands of miles each year for this.